AA Essential

Italian

for kids

AA Publishing

About this book

Jane Wightwick
had the idea

Wina Gunn
wrote the pages

Leila Gaafar (aged 10)
drew the first pictures in
each chapter

Robert Bowers
(not aged 10) drew the
other pictures, and
designed the book

Marc Vitale
did the Italian stuff

Important things that
must be included

Distributed in the United Kingdom by
AA Publishing, Norfolk House, Priestley Road, Basingstoke,
Hampshire RG24 9NY

© **g-and-w PUBLISHING 2001**

A CIP catalogue record for this book is available from the
British Library

ISBN: 0 7495 3039 1

Published by **AA Publishing** (a trading name of Automobile
Association Developments Limited, whose registered office is
Norfolk House, Priestley Road, Basingstoke, Hampshire RG24
9NY. Registered number 1878835)

Printed and bound by **G. Canale & C. S.P.A.**, Torino, Italy

Cover design by **Joshua Smith Graphics**

What's inside

Making friends

How to be cool with the gang

Wanna play?

Our guide to joining in everything from hide-and-seek to the latest electronic game

Feeling hungry

Order your favourite junk or go local

Looking good

Make sure you keep up with all those essential fashions

Hanging out

At the pool, beach or theme park – don't miss out on the action

Pocket money

Spend it here!

Grown-up talk

blah!
blah!
blah!
blah!

If you really, really have to!

Extra bits

All the handy stuff – numbers, months, dates, days of the week

MAKING FRIENDS

me
io ⬥ eeyoh

my snake
il mio serpente
⬥ eel meeyo
sairpentay

my friend
il mio amico
⬥ eel meeyo
ameekoh

my friend
la mia amica
⬥ la meeya
ameekah

my dog
il mio cane
⬥ eel meeyo kanay

my big brother
il mio fratello grande
🗨 eel meeyo fratel-loh granday

grandpa
nonno
🗨 non-noh

grandma
nonna
🗨 non-nah

dad
papà
🗨 pa-pah

mum
mamma
🗨 mam-mah

my little sister
la mia sorellina
🗨 la meeya sorel-leenah

Step this way...

stepfather/stepmother
patrigno/matrigna
🗨 patreenio/matreenia

step-son/
step-daughter
figliastro/figliastra
🗨 feelyeeastroh/
feelyeeastrah

step-brother/step-sister
fratellastro/sorellastra
🗨 fratel-lastroh/sorel-lastrah

Hi!
Ciao!
👄 chee-ow

What's your name?
Come ti chiami?
👄 komay tee kee-amee

My name's ...
Mi chiamo ...
👄 mee kee-amoh

Are you OK?
Stai bene?
👄 sty baynay

Cool, and you?
Benissimo, e tu?
👄 baynees-seemoh ay too

The word **ciao** means "hello" <u>and</u> "goodbye" – it's such a famous word you might already use it with your English friends. You can say **Ciao, come va?** (*chee-ow, komay vah*, "Hi, how's it going?") or **Ciao, ci vediamo!** (*chee-ow, chee vaydee-amoh*, "Bye, see you later!")

8

Where are you from?
Da dove vieni?
👄 dah dovay veeaynee

from England
dall'Inghilterra
👄 dal-lingilter-ra

from Ireland
dall'Irlanda
👄 dal-leerlanda

from Scotland
dalla Scozia
👄 dal-la skotseea

from the U.S.
dagli Stati Uniti
👄 dalyee statee uneetee

from Wales
dal Galles
👄 dal gal-les

I remember the Gauls. We were always fighting them. Tough nuts to crack!

9

How old are you?

Quanti anni hai?

👄 kwantee an-nee eye

12 years old

Dodici anni

👄 dodeechee an-nee

Happy birthday!

Buon compleanno!

👄 boo-on komplayan-no

What's your star sign?

Di che segno sei?

👄 dee kay sayneeo say

When's your birthday?

Quando è il tuo compleanno?

👄 kwando ay eel too-o komplayan-no

What do Italian children play at birthday parties?

Pasta parcel

Star Signs

AQUARIUS
Jan. 21 – Feb. 19
Acquario ~ ak-kwareoh

PISCES
Feb. 20 – Mar. 20
Pesci ~ payshi

ARIES
Mar. 21 – Apr. 20
Ariete ~ aree-aytay

TAURUS
Apr. 21 – May 21
Toro ~ toroh

GEMINI
May 22 – June 21
Gemelli ~ jaymel-lee

CANCER
June 22 – July 23
Cancro ~ kankroh

LEO
July 24 – Aug. 23
Leone ~ layonay

VIRGO
Aug. 24 – Sep. 23
Vergine ~ vairjeenay

LIBRA
Sep. 24 – Oct. 23
Bilancia ~ beelancheea

SCORPIO
Oct. 24 – Nov. 22
Scorpione ~ skorpeeonay

SAGITTARIUS
Nov. 23 – Dec. 21
Sagittario ~ sajeet-tareeo

CAPRICORN
Dec. 22 – Jan. 20
Capricorno ~ kapreecorno

12

football
il calcio
🗣 kalchee-oh

rollerskating/ rollerblading
il pattinaggio
🗣 pat-teenaj-jeeoh

music
la musica
🗣 moozikah

electronic games
i giochi elettronici
🗣 ee jee-okee aylet-tr-roneechee

tv
la tele
🗣 la taylay

comics
i fumetti
🗣 ee foomayt-tee

teddies
gli orsacchiotti
🗣 lyee orsak-kiot-tee

school
la scuola
🗣 la skwolah

spiders
i ragni
🗣 ee ranyee

13

What's ...?
Qual è ...?
👄 kwalay

your favourite group
il tuo complesso preferito
👄 eel too-oh komples-soh pray-fayreetoh

your favourite colour
il tuo colore preferito
👄 eel too-oh koloray pray-fayreetoh

→ Page 51

your favourite food
il tuo cibo preferito
👄 eel too-oh cheeboh pray-fayreetoh

your favourite team
la tua squadra preferita
👄 la too-ah skwadra pray-fayreetah

animal

your favourite animal
il tuo animale preferito
👄 eel too-oh aneemalay pray-fayreetoh

14

dog
il cane
👄 eel kanay

cat
il gatto
👄 eel gat-toh

guinea-pig
il porcellino d'India
👄 eel porchel-leenoh
deendeea

snake
il serpente
👄 eel sairpayntay

hamster
il criceto
👄 eel crichaytoh

budgie
il pappagallino
👄 eel pap-pagal-leenoh

My little doggy goes *"bau bau"*!

An Italian doggy doesn't say "woof, woof", it says **bau, bau** (*baoo, baoo*). An Italian bird says **pio, pio** (*pee-o, pee-o*) and a "cock-a-doodle-do" in Italian chicken-speak is **chicchirichì** (*keek-kee ree-kee*). But a cat does say "miao" and a cow "moo" whether they're speaking Italian or English!

15

Talk about school (if you can bear it)

geography
la geografia
lah jayografeea

art
l'educazione artistica
laydookatseeonay arteesteekah

PE
l'educazione fisica
laydookatseeona feezeekah

Italian
l'italiano
leetaleeano

Italian
m.smith
form 2b

maths
la matematica
la matimateekah

English
l'inglese
leenglayzay

music
la musica
la moozeekah

English
m.smith
I love Sandra

science
le scienze
👄 lay shee-enzay

history
la storia
👄 la storeeah

Way unfair!

Italian children hardly ever have to wear uniform to school nowadays (but in primary school they used to wear overalls, white with a big blue bow for girls and blue with a big white bow for boys!). Summer holidays are very long, sometimes even up to 12 weeks. But before you turn green with envy, you might not like the dreaded **ripetizioni** (*reepay-teetsee-onee*) or "vacation classes", which you have to take if you fail your exams at the end of the year. And if your marks are really bad the teachers could make you repeat the whole year with your little sister!

Gossip

Can you keep a secret?
Sai mantenere un segreto?
🔊 sah-ee mantaynayray oon saygretoh

An OK guy/An OK girl
Un tipo simpatico/Una tipa simpatica
🔊 oon teepo seempateekoh/ oona teepa seempateekah

He's nutty/She's nutty!
È uno svitato/ È una svitata!
🔊 ay oono sveetatoh/ ay oona sveetatah

svitato means "unscrewed"!

Do you have a boyfriend (a girlfriend)?

Ce l'hai il ragazzo (la ragazza)?
🔊 chay laee eel ragatsoh (lah ragatsah)

What a bossy-boots!
Che prepotente!
🔊 kay praypotayntay

What a misery-guts!
Che lagna!
🔊 kay laneea

You won't make many friends saying this!

Bog off!
Levati dai piedi!
⌇ layvatee die peeaydee

Shut up!
Sta' zitto!
⌇ stah dzeet-toh

That means "get off my feet"!

If you're fed up with someone, and you want to say something like "you silly …!" or "you stupid …!" you can start with **testa di …** (which actually means "head of …") and add anything you like. The most common are:

or …

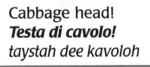

Cabbage head!
Testa di cavolo!
taystah dee kavoloh

Turnip head!
Testa di rapa!
taystah dee rapah

Take your pick. You could also start with **pezzo di …** ("piece of …") and say **pezzo d'idiota!** (*paytso deedee-otah*). You don't need a translation here, do you?

Saying goodbye

Here's my address
Ecco il mio indirizzo
👄 ekko eel meeo
eendeereetso

What's your address?
Qual è il tuo indirizzo?
👄 kwalay eel too-oh
eendeereetso

Come to visit me
Vieni a travarmi
👄 vee-aynee ah
trovarmee

Write to me soon
Scrivimi presto
👄 skreeveemee praystoh

Have a good trip!
Buon viaggio!
👄 bwon veeajeeoh

Bye!
Ciao!
👄 chee-ow

21

l'elastico
👄 laylasteeko

il ping-pong
👄 eel peeng pong

la campana
la kampanah

il Gameboy
eel gameboy

le biglie
lay beelyeeay

lo yo-yó
loh "yo-yo"

WANNA PLAY?

23

Do you want to play ...?
Vuoi giocare ...?
🗣 voo-oi jokaray

... table football?
... a calcetto?
🗣 ah kal-chayt-toh

... cards?
... a carte?
🗣 ah kartay

... on the computer?
... al computer?
🗣 al komputer

... hangman?
... all'impiccato?
🗣 al-leempeek-katoh

... hide-and-seek?
... a nascondino?
🗣 ah naskondeenoh

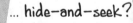

... catch?
... a pallone?
🗣 ah pal-lonay

Fancy a game of **leap the foal** or **pretty statues**?

In Italy, tag is called **chiapparello** (*kiap-parel-loh*), which sort of means "catchy-poos"! And instead of leap frog, Italian children play leap "foal" – **la cavallina** (*lah caval-leenah*). Another very popular game is **belle statuine** (*bellah statoo-eenah*) or "pretty statues", which is similar to "big bad wolf". When someone is standing around doing nothing, Italians will often ask "Are you playing pretty statues?" – **Fai la bella statuina?** (*faee lah bellah statoo-eenah*).

Make yourself heard

You're it!
Stai sotto tu!
👄 sty sot-to too

Who's winning?
Chi vince?
👄 kee veenchay

Race you?
Facciamo una corsa?
👄 facheeamoh oona korsah

I'm first
Sono primo io (boy)
Sono prima io (girl)
👄 sonoh preemoh eeo
   sonoh preemah eeo

27

Electronic games

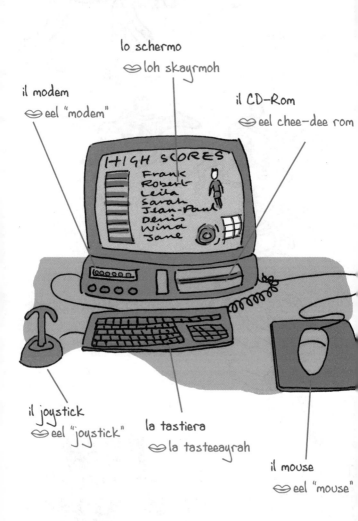

lo schermo
👄 loh skayrmoh

il modem
👄 eel "modem"

il CD-Rom
👄 eel chee-dee rom

HIGH SCORES
Frank
Robert
Leila
Sarah
Jean-Paul
Denis
Nina
Jane

il joystick
👄 eel "joystick"

la tastiera
👄 la tasteeayrah

il mouse
👄 eel "mouse"

What do I do?
Che devo fare?
👄 kay dayvoh faray

Show me
Fammi vedere
👄 fam-mee vaydayray

Am I dead?
Sono morto?
👄 sonoh mortoh

Shoot-em-up!
Spara!
👄 sparah

How many lives do I have?
Quante vite ho?
👄 kwantay veetay oh

How many levels are there?
Quanti livelli ci sono?
👄 kwantee leevayl-lee chee sonoh

29

Non couch-potato activities!

tennis
il tennis
👄 eel ten–nees

trampolining
il trampolino
👄 eel trampoleenoh

bowling
il bowling
👄 eel booleeng

swimming
il nuoto
👄 eel noo–oto

hockey
l'hockey
👄 lok-kay

gymnastics
la ginnastica
👄 la jeen-nasteekah

ballet
la danza classica
👄 la dantsa klas-seekah

basketball la pallacanestro
👄 la pal-lakanaystroh

and, of course, we haven't forgotten "*il calcio*" ... (P.T.O.)

footy

boots
gli scarponcini
👄 lyee skarponcheenee

shin-pads
i parastinchi
👄 ee parasteenkee

ref
l'arbitro
👄 larbeetroh

football kit
la divisa da calcio
👄 lah deeveezah dah kalcheeo

Good save!
Ben parato!
👄 ben paratoh

crossbar
la traversa
👄 la travayrsah

goalpost
il palo
👄 eel palo

goal
la porta
👄 la portah

goalie
il portiere
👄 eel porteeayray

Pass!
Passa!
👄 pas-sah

32

33

Keeping the others in line

Not like that!
Cosi no!
👄 kozee noh

You cheat!
Sei un imbroglione! (boys only)
Sei un'imbrogliona! (girls only)
👄 say oon eembrolyee-onay
say oon eembrolyee-onah

I'm not playing anymore
Non gioco più
👄 non jeeoko peeoo

It's not fair!
Non vale!
👄 non valay

Stop it!
Smettila!
👄 smayt-teela

34

Impress your Italian friends with this!

Show off to your new Italian friends by practising this **scioglilingua** (*shee-olyeleen-gooa*), or tongue twister:

Sopra la panca la capra campa, sotto la panca la capra crepa.

soprah la pankah la kaprah kampah, sot-toh la pankah la kaprah kraypah

(This means "On the bench the goat lives, under the bench the goat dies.")

Then see if they can do as well with this English one:

"She sells sea shells on the sea shore, but the shells she sells aren't sea shells, I'm sure."

For a rainy day

pack of cards
mazzo di carte
🗣 matso dee kartay

my deal/your deal
faccio io le carte/
fai tu le carte
🗣 facheeo eeo lay kartay/
faee too lay kartay

king
il re
🗣 eel ray

queen
la regina
🗣 la rayjeenah

jack
il fante
🗣 eel fantay

joker
il jolly
🗣 eel jol-lee

fiori
🗣 feeoree

cuori
🗣 koo-oree

picche
🗣 peek-kay

quadri
🗣 kwadree

36

Do you have the ace of swords?!

You will probably see Italian children playing with a different pack of cards. There are only 40 cards instead of 52 and the suits are also different. Instead of clubs, spades, diamonds and hearts, there are gold coins (**denari**), swords (**spade**), cups (**coppe**) and sticks (**bastoni**).

chessboard
la scacchiera
👄 la skak-keeayrah

l'alfiere
👄 lalfeeayray

il cavallo
👄 eel kaval-loh

il pedone
👄 eel paydonay

la torre
👄 lah torray

la regina
👄 lah rayjeeanah

il re
👄 eel ray

37

FEELING HUNGRY

hamburger
l'hamburger
👄 lamboorgir

chips
le patate fritte
👄 lay patatay
freet-tay

ice-cream
il gelato
👄 eel jaylat...

coke
la cola
👄 la kolah

38

creme caramel
il crème caramel
👄 eel krem karamel

squid
i calamari
👄 ee kalamaree

mussels
le cozze
👄 lay kotsay

orange juice
la spremuta d'arancia
👄 la spraymootah
d'arancheeah

FEELING HUNGRY

39

Grub

I'm starving

Ho una fame da lupo

👄 oh oona famay dah loopoh

il lupo

That means "I have the hunger of a wolf!"

Please can I have ...

Mi dà ...

👄 mee dah

... a chocolate bun

... un pasticcino al cioccolato

👄 oon pasteech–cheeno al chok–kolatoh

... a croissant

... un cornetto

👄 oon cornayt–toh

... a puff pastry

... una pasta sfoglia

👄 oonah pasta sfolyah

40

... a slice of pizza
... un pezzo di pizza
 oon paytso dee peetsa

a sandwich
un tramezzino
 oon tramay—dzeeno

a pizza pastie
un calzone
 oon caltsonay

Take-away pizza in Italy is often sold **al taglio** (*al talyee-oh*), which means it is cut into rectangular slices from a large baking sheet … and you can buy as big a piece as you like! Another great midday snack is a **calzone** (*caltsonay*), which is a round pizza folded in half to look like a pastie, with all the juicy bits inside!

In the winter, you can buy bags of delicious roasted chestnuts from street sellers, hot and ready to eat!

a bag of chestnuts
un cartoccio di castagne
 oon kartocheeo dee kastaneeay

If you want something really cold and slushy in the summer you can ask for **una granita** (oona graneetah), which is crushed ice with fruit juice or squash.

water
acqua
akkwah

a milkshake
un frullato
oon frool-latoh

a squash
uno sciroppo
oonoh sheerop-poh

If you're really lucky you might go to Italy during **Carnevale** in February. Adults and kids dress up in the wierdest costumes and everyone goes loopy for a few days. There are lots of special sticky cakes like *frappe* (*frappay*): big pastry bows dipped in icing sugar; and **castagnole** (*kastanyolay*): delicious fried balls of pastry covered in sugar.

You: Can I have some castagnole, Mum?

Mum: No. They'll make you fat and rot your teeth.

You: But I think it's good to experience a foreign culture through authentic local food.

Mum: Oh, all right then.

How did you like it?

That's lovely
È buonissimo
👄 ay boo-onees-
seemoh

That's gorgeous
È squisito
👄 ay skweezeetoh

I don't like that
Non mi piace
👄 non mee pee-achay

I'm stuffed
Sono pieno (boys)
Sono piena (girls)
👄 sonoh peeaynoh
sonoh peeaynah

I can't eat that
Questo non lo posso mangiare
👄 kwaysto non lo pos-soh
manjeearay

That's gross
Che schifo
👄 kay skeefoh

Pasta Pasta Pasta!

Italians, especially those from Naples, claim to have invented pasta (we know it really grows on trees!). There are lots of different types of pasta and just as many, if not more, different sauces to go with them, including a sauce made with squid ink! You have probably heard of **spaghetti** and **tagliatelle**, but what about these:

penne (quills)

farfalle (butterflies)

lumache (snails!)

ruote (wheels)

stelline (little stars)

nail varnish
lo smalto per le unghie
🗣 loh smaltoh pair lay oongeeay

headband
il cerchietto
🗣 eel chirkeeayt-t...

bracelets
i braccialetti
🗣 ee brach–
chalaytee

braid
la treccia
🗣 la traycr...

crop top
la camicetta
🗣 la
kameechayt-tak

belt
la cintura
🗣 la cheentoorah

miniskirt
la minigonna
🗣 la meeneegon-nar

shoes
le scarpe
🗣 lay skarpay

bike
la bici
🗣 la beechee

LOOKING GOOD

46

T-shirt
la maglietta
la malyeeayt-tah

cap
il berretto
eel ber-rayt-toh

tattoo
il tatuaggio
eel tatooaj-jeeo

jeans
i jeans
ee jeens

il walkman
eel "walkman"

skateboard
lo skate-board
loh "skateboard"

trainers
gli scarponcini
lyee skarponcheenee

LOOKING GOOD

47

She's got an orange hair!

There are lots of double letters in Italian. Saying the double letter properly can be very important. For example, a hat is **un cappello** (*oon cap-payl-loh*), with two "p"s, but a hair is **un capello** (*oon capayl-lo*).

spotty
a pois
👄 ah pooah

flowery
a fiori
👄 ah feeoree

frilly
a fronzoli
👄 ah frondzolee

glittery
luccicante
👄 luch-cheekantay

stripey
a strisce
👄 ah streeshay

49

jeans
i jeans
👄 ee jeens

T-shirt
la maglietta
👄 lah malyeeayt-ta

sweatshirt
la felpa
👄 la faylpah

trainers
gli scarponcini
👄 lyee skarponcheenee

dress
il vestito
👄 eel vaysteetoh

skirt
la gonna
👄 la gon-nah

trousers
i pantaloni
👄 ee pantalor

football shirt
la maglietta da calcio
👄 lah malyeeayt-tah da calcheeo

shorts
i pantaloncini
👄 ee pantaloncheenee

shoes
le scarpe
👄 lay skarpay

Colour this page yourself
(you can't expect us to do everything!)

colours
i colori
👄 ee coloree

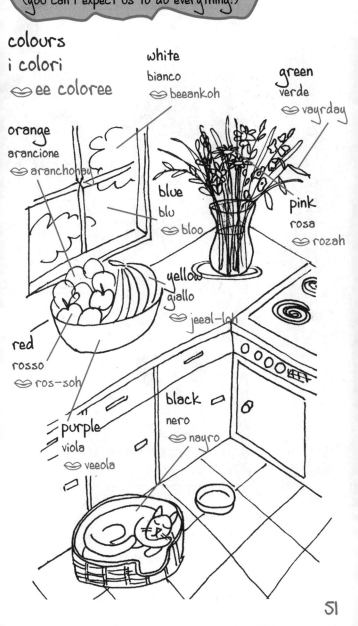

white
bianco
👄 beeankoh

green
verde
👄 vayrday

orange
arancione
👄 aranchohnay

blue
blu
👄 bloo

pink
rosa
👄 rozah

yellow
giallo
👄 jeeal-loh

red
rosso
👄 ros-soh

black
nero
👄 nayro

purple
viola
👄 veeola

What shall we do?
Che facciamo?
 kay facheeamoh

Can I come?
Vengo anch'io?
vayngo ankeeoh

Where do you lot hang out?
Dove v'incontrate?
dovay veenkontratay

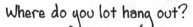

That's really wicked
Che forte
kay fortay

I'm (not) allowed
(Non) mi lasciano
(non) mee lasheeanoh

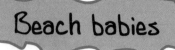

Beach babies

Can I borrow this?
Me lo presti?
👄 may loh praystee

Let's hit the beach
Tutti al mare
👄 toot–tee al marae

Is this your bucket?
È tuo questo secchiello?
👄 ay too–o kwestoh saykeeayl–lo

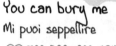

You can bury me
Mi puoi seppellire
👄 mee poo–oee sayp–payl–leeray

Stop throwing sand!
Smetti di tirare la sabbia!
👄 smayt–tee dee teeraray la sab–beeah

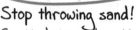

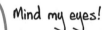

Mind my eyes!
Non mi buttare la sabbia negli occhi!
👄 non mee boot–taray la sab–beea nelyee ok–kee

56

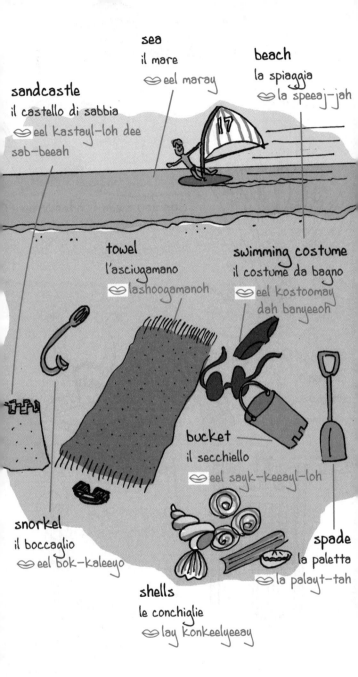

sea
il mare
eel maray

beach
la spiaggia
la speeaj-jah

sandcastle
il castello di sabbia
eel kastayl-loh dee sab-beeah

towel
l'asciugamano
lashoogamanoh

swimming costume
il costume da bagno
eel kostoomay dah banyeeoh

bucket
il secchiello
eel sayk-keeayl-loh

snorkel
il boccaglio
eel bok-kaleeyo

spade
la paletta
la palayt-tah

shells
le conchiglie
lay konkeelyeeay

57

It's going swimmingly!

How to make a splash in Italian!

PLUF

Let's hit the swimming pool
Tutti in piscina
👄 toot-tee een peesheen

Can you swim (underwater)?
Sai nuotare (sott'acqua)?
👄 saee nwotaray (sot-takwah)

Me too/I can't
Anch'io/Io no
👄 ankeeo/eeo noh

Can you dive?
Ti sai tuffare?
👄 tee sah-ee toof-faray

I'm getting changed
Mi sto cambiando
👄 mee stoh kambeeandoh

Can you do ...?
Sai fare ...?
👄 sah-ee faray

... back stroke
il dorso
👄 eel dorsoh

... butterfly
la farfalla
👄 la farfal-la

... crawl
il crawl
👄 eel "crawl"

... breast stroke
la rana   👄 la ranah

[which means "the frog", and, let's face it, that's what you look like!]

slide
lo scivolo
👄 loh sheevoloh

goggles
gli occhialetti
👄 lyee ok-keealayt-tee

59

Downtown

Italy has a high-speed train called the **Pendolino**, which means 'leaning over', because the carriages lean to the side when it speeds round bends. Persuade your parents to try it – it's better than a rollercoaster at the fun fair!

Do you know the way?
Sai la strada?
🗢 sah-ee la stradah

Is it far?
È lontano? 🗢 ay lontanoh

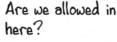
Are we allowed in here?
Possiamo entrare?
🗢 pos-seeamoh ayntraray

Let's ask
Chiediamo
🗢 kyee-aydeeamoh

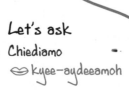

60

playground
il parco giochi
👄 eel parko jeeokee

slide
lo scivolo
👄 lo sheevolo

park il parco 👄 eel parko

swings
le altalene
👄 lay altalaynay

bus l'autobus
👄 laootoboos

car la macchina
👄 lah mak-keenah

The "proper" Italian word for car is **automobile** (*aootomobeelay*) but you'll look much cooler if you say **macchina** (*mak-keenah*) or, if the car has seen better days, **macinino** (*makeeneenoh*). Use the cooler short words instead of those long untrendy ones the adults will try and make you say: **bici** (*beechee*) instead of **bicicletta**, **moto** instead of **motocicletta** and **bus** (*boos*) instead of **autobus**.

Picnics

I hate wasps
Odio le vespe
👄 odeeo lay vayspay

Move over!
Fatti più in là!
👄 fat-tee peeoo een lah

bread
il pane 👄 eel panay

Let's sit here
Sediamoci qui
👄 saydeeamochee kwee

napkin
il tovagliolo
👄 eel tovalyeeolo

ham
il prosciutto
👄 eel proshoot-to

cheese
il formaggio
👄 eel formaj-jeeo

yoghurt
lo yogurt
👄 loh yogoort

crisps
le patatine
👄 lay patateenay

62

drinks
le bibite
👄 lay beebeetay

knife
il coltello
👄 eel koltayl-lo

spoon
il cucchiaio
👄 eel kuk-keeayo

fork
la forchetta
👄 la forkayt-tah

wasps
le vespe
👄 lay vayspay

bees
le api
👄 lay apee

bzzzz

ants
le formiche
👄 lay formeekay

All the fun of the fair

helter-skelter
lo scivolo
🗨 loh sheevolo

big wheel
la ruota panoramica
🗨 la rwotah panorameeka

house of mirrors
la casa degli specchi
🗨 la kasah delyee spaykee

dodge-ems
l'autoscontro
🗨 laootoskontro

Let's try this
Andiamo su questo
🗨 andeeamo soo kwesto

roundabout
la giostra
👄 la jeeostra

It's (too) fast
Va (troppo) forte
👄 Vah trop-po fortay

That's for babies
Quello è per i bambini
👄 kwayl-lo ay payr ee
bambeenee

WATER CHUTE

SPOOKY HAUNTED HOUSE?

Do you get wet here?
Qui ci si bagna?
👄 kwee chee see banya

I'm not going on my own
Da solo/a non ci vado
👄 dah solo/a non chee vado

65

Spend it here

sweets
le caramelle
🗣 lay karamayl-lay

T-shirts
le magliette
🗣 lay malyeeayt-tay

toys
i giocattoli
🗣 ee jeeokat-tolee

shop assistant
il commesso
🗣 eel kom-may-

POCKET MONEY

books
i libri
👄 ee leebree

il mobile
👄 eel "mobile"

pencils
le matite
👄 lay mateetay

POCKET MONEY

67

What does that sign say?

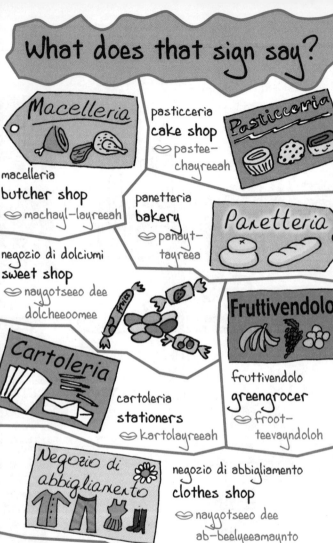

Macelleria

macelleria
butcher shop
👄 machayl–layreeah

pasticceria
cake shop
👄 pastee–chayreeah

Pasticceria

panetteria
bakery
👄 panayt–tayreea

Paretteria

negozio di dolciumi
sweet shop
👄 naygotseeo dee dolcheeoomee

Fruttivendolo

fruttivendolo
greengrocer
👄 froot–teevayndoloh

Cartoleria

cartoleria
stationers
👄 kartolayreeah

Negozio di abbigliamento

negozio di abbigliamento
clothes shop
👄 naygotseeo dee ab–beelyeeamaynto

Money talk

Italian money is **lire** (*leeray*).
Coins: 50, 100, 200, 500, 1000 lire
Notes: 1000, 2000, 5000, 10,000, 50,000 and 100,000
As you can see, you have to spend lots of **lire** to buy
anything at all, so don't think you're rich if you have a
1000 lire note. It may be just enough to buy a few
sweets for you and a couple of friends.

Do you have some dosh?
Ce l'hai qualche soldo?
👄 chay lie kwalkay soldo

I'm skint
Sono al verde
👄 sono al vayrday

I'm loaded
Sono ricco sfondato
👄 sono reek-ko sfondato

Here you go
Tieni
👄 teeaynee

Can you lend me five thousand lire? Mi presti cinquemila lire?
👄 mee praystee chinkway meelah leeray

No way!
Neanche per sogno!
👄 nayankay payr sonyeeo

That's a bargain
È un affare
👄 ay oon af-faray

10,000

It's a rip off!
Questi ti spellano!
👄 kwaystee tee spayl-lanoh

Sweet heaven!

I love this shop
Amo questo negozio
👄 amo kwesto naygotseeo

Let's get some sweets
Prendiamo delle caramelle
👄 prayndeeamo dayllay karamayl-lay

Let's get an ice cream
Prendiamo un gelato
👄 prayndeeamo oon jaylatoh

lollipops
lecca lecca
👄 lek-kah lek-kah
[that means "lick-lick"!]

a bar of chocolate
una tavoletta di cioccolata
👄 oona tavolayt-tah dee chok-kolatah

chewing gum
gomma da masticare
👄 gom-mah dah masteekaray

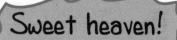

If you really want to look Italian (but end up with lots of fillings) try these:

baci Perugina
(bachee peroo-jeenah)

The most famous Italian chocolate has to be **baci Perugina** (literally "kisses"), balls of chocolate and nuts wrapped in silver paper with little romantic messages for that boy or girl you fancy!

carbone di zucchero
(carbonay dee dzook-kayro)!

Sugar coal. On 6th January, the Epiphany, Italian kids get presents, but those who have been naughty get coal! Actually this is black coal-shaped candy – phew!

pecorelle di zucchero
(paykorayl-lay dee dzook-kayro).

Forget the Easter eggs, try some 'sugar lambs'!

Kinder sorpresa
(kinder sorpraysah)

Your probably know these "Kinder Surprise" chocolate eggs with wicked little toys, but did you know they come from Italy?

Other things you could buy
(that won't rot your teeth!)

What are you getting?
Tu che prendi?
👄 too kay prayndee

That toy, please
Quel giocattolo, per favore
👄 kwayl jeeokat-toloh
payr favoray

Two postcards, please
Due cartoline, per favore
👄 dooay
kartoleenay
payr favoray

How much is that?
Quanto costa?
👄 kwanto kostah

This is rubbish
Questa è robaccia
👄 kwesta ay
robach-cha

This is cool
Questo è
eccezionale
👄 kwesto ay echetseeonalay

72

... colouring pencils
... delle matite colorate
😊 dellay mateetay coloratay

I'm getting ...
Io prendo ... 😊 eeo prendoh

... stamps
... dei francobolli
😊 day franko-bol-lee

... felt tip pens
... dei pennarelli
😊 day pen-narel-lee

... a pen
... una penna
😊 oona pen-nah

... a cassette
... una cassetta
😊 oona kas-set-tah

... a CD
... un CD
😊 oon cheedee

... comics
... dei fumetti
😊 day foomayt-tee

Italian kids, and adults, have always been mad about Disney comics. But did you know that most of the characters have Italian names you wouldn't recognise? Mickey Mouse and Minnie Mouse are **Topolino** and **Topolina** ("little mouse"), Goofy is **Pippo**, Donald Duck is **Paperino** ("little duck") and Huey, Dewey and Louie are **Qui, Quo, Qua**!

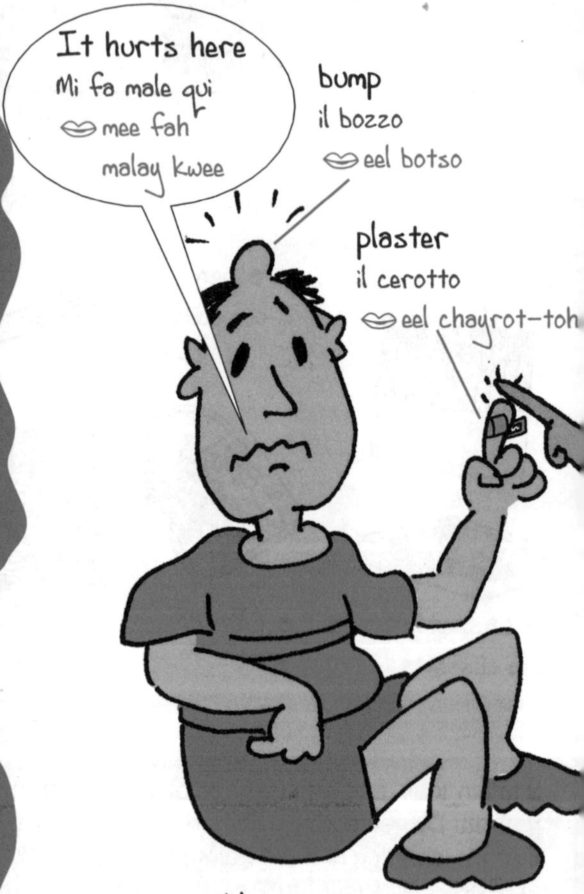

child
bambino/bambina
bambeenoh (boy) / bambeenah (girl)

Help!

Something has broken
Si è rotto qualcosa
👄 see ay rot-to kwalkozah

Please
Per favore
👄 payr favoray

Can you help me?
Può aiutarmi?
👄 poo-o aeeootarmee

Where's the letter box?
Dov'è la buca delle lettere?
👄 dovay lah booka dayl-lay layt-tayray

Where are the toilets?
Dov'è il bagno?
👄 dovay eel banyeeo

I can't manage it
Non ci riesco

🗨 non chee ree-aysko

Could you pass me that?
Mi passi quello?

🗨 mee pas-see kwayl-lo

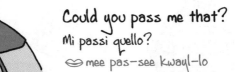

What's the time?
Che ore sono?

🗨 kay oray sonoh

Come and see
Vieni a vedere

🗨 veeaynee ah vaydayray

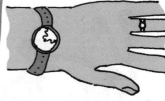

May I look on your watch?
Mi fa vedere sul suo orologio

🗨 mee fah vaydayray sool
soo-o orolojeeo

77

Lost for words

... my ticket
... il mio biglietto
👄 eel meeo
    bilyee-ayt-to

I've lost ...
Ho perso ...
👄 oh payrso

... my bike
... la mia bici
👄 lah meeah beechee

... my parents
... i miei genitori
👄 ee meeay
    jayneetoree

... my shoes
... le mie scarpe
👄 lay meeay skarpay

... my money
... i miei soldi
👄 ee meeay soldee

... my jumper
... la mia maglia
👄 lah meeah malyeeah

... my watch
... il mio orologio
👄 eel meeoh orolojeeo

... my jacket
... la mia giacca
👄 lah meeah jeeak-kah

79

ADULTS ONLY!

Show this page to adults who can't seem to make themselves clear (it happens). They will point to a phrase, you read what they mean and you should all understand each other perfectly.

Non ti preoccupare
Don't worry

Siediti qui
Sit down here

Come ti chiami di nome e di cognome?
What's your name and surname?

Quanti anni hai?
How old are you?

Di dove sei?
Where are you from?

Dove sei alloggiato/a?
Where are you staying?

Cos'è che ti fa male?
Where does it hurt?

Sei allergico/a a qualcosa?
Are you allergic to anything?

È proibito
It's forbidden

Devi essere accompagnato/a da un adulto
You have to have an adult with you

Vado a cercare qualcuno che parli l'inglese
I'll get someone who speaks English

Knock, knock.

Who's there?

Uno.

Uno who?

Unos where I got this crummy joke!

uno 👄 oonoh

due 👄 doo-ay

tre 👄 tray

quattro 👄 kwat-troh

cinque 👄 cheenkway

sei
👄 say

sette
👄 sayt-tay

otto
👄 ot-toh

nove
👄 novay

dieci
👄 deeaychee

undici
👄 oondeechee

dodici
👄 dodeechee

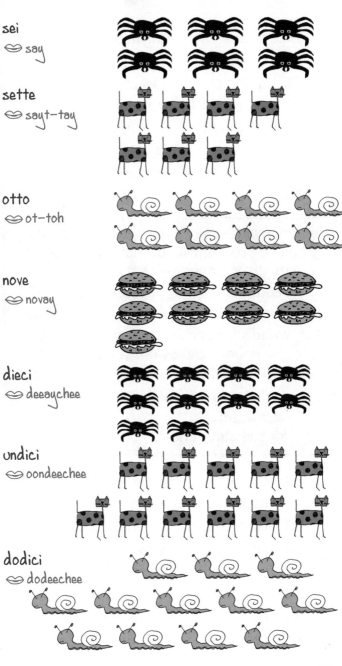

13	tredici	*traydeechee*
14	quattordici	*kwat-tordeechee*
15	quindici	*kweendeechee*
16	sedici	*saydeechee*
17	diciassette	*deechas-set-tay*
18	diciotto	*deechot-toh*
19	diciannove	*dechan-novay*
20	venti	*ventee*

If you want to say "twenty-two", "sixty-five" and so on, you can just put the two numbers together like you do in English:

22	**ventidue**	*venteedooay*
65	**sessantacinque**	*sess-santacheenkway*

This works except if you're saying "twenty-one", "sixty-one" and so on. Then you need to remove the final letter from the first number:

21	**ventuno** (not **ventiuno**)	*ventoonoh*
61	**sessantuno** (not **sessantauno**)	*sess-santoonoh*

30	trenta	*trentah*
40	quaranta	*kwarantah*
50	cinquanta	*cheengkwantah*
60	sessanta	*saysenta*
70	settanta	*set-tantah*
80	ottanta	*ot-tantah*
90	novanta	*novantah*
100	cento	*chentoh*

You might notice that Italians wave their hands a lot when they speak. What you won't realise is that not all flapping and waving means the same. Try looking out for some of these:

"What do you want?"

"Say that again"

"Are you crazy?"

"He's changed his mind"

March	marzo	*martsoh*
April	aprile	*apreelay*
May	maggio	*madjoh*

June	giugno	*joonyoh*
July	luglio	*loolyoh*
August	agosto	*agosstoh*

September	settembre	*set-tembray*
October	ottobre	*ot-tobray*
November	novembre	*novembray*

December	dicembre	*deechembray*
January	gennaio	*jen-nayoh*
February	febbraio	*feb-brayoh*

primavera   *preemavayrah*

SPRING

estate   *esstatay*

SUMMER

autunno   *owtoon-noh*

AUTUMN

inverno   *eenvernoh*

WINTER

Monday	lunedì	*loonaydee*
Tuesday	martedì	*martaydee*
Wednesday	mercoledì	*merkolaydee*
Thursday	giovedì	*jovaydee*
Friday	venerdì	*vaynerdee*
Saturday	sabato	*sabatoh*
Sunday	domenica	*domayneekah*

By the way, school starts at around 8.30 a.m. for most children in Italy and ends around 1.00 p.m., but they also have to go to school on Saturday morning.

Good times

It's ...
Sono ...
👄 sonoh

(five) o'clock
le (cinque)
👄 lay (cheenkway)

quarter past (two)
le (due) e un quarto
👄 lay (dooay) ay oon kwarto

quarter to (four)
le (quattro) meno un quarto
👄 lay (kwat-troh) maynoh
oon kwartoh

half past (three)
le (tre) e mezzo
👄 lay (tray) ay medzoh

90

five past (ten)
le (dieci) e cinque
❰ lay (deeaychee)
   ay cheenkway

twenty past (eleven)
le (undici) e venti
❰ lay (oondeechee)
   ay ventee

ten to (four)
le (quattro) meno dieci
❰ lay (kwat-troh) maynoh
   deeaychee

twenty to (six)
le (sei) meno venti
❰ lay (say) maynoh vayntee

W atch out for "one o'clock". It's a bit different from the other times. If you want to say "It's one o'clock" you have to say **È l'una** (*ay loonah*). "It's half past one" is **È l'una e mezza** (*ay loonah ay medzah*), and so on.

morning
la mattina

👄 lah mat–teenah

midday
mezzogiorno

👄 medzojorrnoh

afternoon
il pomeriggio

👄 eel pomayreedjoh

midnight
mezzanotte

👄 medzanot–tay

evening
la sera

👄 lah sayrah

92

93

Weather wise

Can we go out?
Possiamo uscire?
👄 pos–seeamoh oosheeray

It's hot
Fa caldo 👄 fah kaldoh

It's cold
Fa freddo
👄 fah frayd–doh

It's a horrible day
Fa cattivo tempo
👄 fa kat–teevoh taympoh

It's raining basins!

When it rains heavily in Italy, people say it's "raining basins": **Piove a catinelle** (*peeovay ah kateenayl–lay*). A well-known saying is **Cielo a pecorelle acqua a catinelle**, or "Lambs in the sky means basins of water"! "Lambs" means little fluffy clouds!

It's windy
C'è vento
👄 chay vayntoh

It's sunny
C'è il sole
👄 chay eel solay

It's snowing
Nevica
👄 nayveekah

It's raining
Piove
👄 peeovay

It's nice
Fa bel tempo
👄 fah bel tempoh

I'm soaked
Sono fradicio
👄 sono fradeecheeo

95